Mostly Human

Sheila Squillante

MOSTLY HUMAN

Editor: Clarinda Harriss
Graphic Design: Ace Kieffer
Cover Art: Kerstin Rünzel

BrickHouse Books, Inc. 2020
306 Suffolk Road
Baltimore, MD 21218

Distributor: Itasca Books, Inc.

ISBN: 978-1-938144-75-2

Printed in the United States of America

for all the gen-x girls who longed to escape

TABLE OF CONTENTS

Round Baby Hangs on No Matter How

Twice your life ago, sat a Round Baby
on the porch of a small yellow house
near the broken side of the Poconos.
Fat stumps of leg poking out from under
the walker, toes gripping purchase
on the urethaned wood of the deck.
Grandparents somewhere,
parents, presumably, too. In the picture,
Baby holds a nubby orange ball. It looks
like a planet. It looks like a tumor. She chews
on it and pulls futilely at the foam. Manual
dexterity comes later. But Baby can already grip
Grandfather's cigar. Origin stories called her
strong. Said she'd hang on no matter
how hard he pulled it away.

> (Under the deck, slick flagstone
> and moss. Earthworms
> and salamanders glinting,
> like stars in the dark woods.)

Round Baby Can't Taste It Yet

Round ball, round Baby. Round with worry. Worry
like a lozenge, lodged in her throat. She can't taste it
yet, but carries it with her, rolls it between legs
splayed open on the floor, on top of polyester
shag carpet. Downstairs orange, cream and black.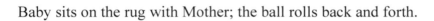
Upstairs blues and greens. When you pass your one
hand over it, fire. The other, water, moss, dark earth.

Baby sits on the rug with Mother; the ball rolls back and forth.

Round Baby Considers the Circle

Other things are round, too. Dimes,
tires, apples, wheel. Some internal organs
take a roundish shape. Liver. Spleen. Dinner
plate. *Marbles don't go in your mouth, Baby.*
Plastic backyard swimming pool. Round.
Grandfather, an enormous white planet,
a grounded sphere. Baby pours buckets
of water over his fat orb head, rubs
his fleshy belly, feels luck's flush.

Round Baby Screams & Runs

Near the porch swing, Baby
plays the toe naming game
with Grandmother. In the alley, Sister
picks up a dead bird by the neck,
offers it to Mother, an oily grey gift.

Years yet before there will be a tomcat
sleeking over counter tops, shitting
in clean laundry and spraying
house guests asleep on the burning shag
downstairs. Years before clarity of mind
and shape. Before she'll see things
as they really are. A breeze pushes
in and every hair on her body zings.
Baby's eye catches a flutter
in the corner under the eaves.

It travels toward her fast and black,
arachnic cloud, massive sun, silken
wheel whining like wind as it comes.
Baby screams and runs for the tool shed,
the swimming pool, the ocean, the woods.
Grandmother's many hands weave a loose
web to grab her, hold her, love her, trap her
here on Earth.

Round Baby Reaches toward Interstitial Space

At Easter time, there is a lengthening. The light
over the earth grows longer. The hyacinth stalks

grow taller until purple and pink nubs rupture.
Baby lengthens, too. Legs and arms and neck.

She feels herself reaching toward interstitial
space. Her head, though, is still a ball.

The kitchen smells of sulfur and vinegar.
Her stained fingers thrum Formica

tabletop. Eggs at least have a shallow end.
Something to interrupt the worry. But balls

roll forever, endless, in every direction.
You have to chase them into the street.

Round Baby Bounces

Bounce, Baby, from room
to room. Living room's white

brick mantelpiece, champagne
carpeting, Naugahyde couch.

Bounce to the bedroom where
Sister sleeps beneath

a window that darkens with vortex,
with birds winging odd geometries.

Bounce into the hallway where
Mother moves you in the storm.

It's tube-shaped and the doors
and windows shut tight behind you.

Father's on the phone, Baby, all the way
from somewhere. He so cares.

The hot wind whines and the cord uncurls
from the kitchen, until it ends, taut

and tethered to Mother's great fear.
When the line goes dead again, she will lay

her body over you while the dark circles in.

Round Baby Pronounces & Proclaims

Baby's a maker.
Fits plastic sticks
into gear wheels.

Wooden dolls
to clamps and dowels.
Press here to open:

Look, she moves her leg!
Baby makes words

in new languages
with her regular
tongue. Strings sounds

like plastic beads from a craft
kit. Shiny balls that scatter
and roll. Bits of import wedged

between nonsense
and noise. Baby pronounces
and proclaims. Undeterred

by syntax, she moves
to her own motions, bleats
beats and buzzings, beautiful

illumined sounds that signal
and suggest.

Round Baby Feels a Strange Breaking

Christmas lights throw shadow
against little plum face. She sits
in the massive oak rocking chair
next to the aluminum tree. Her feet don't reach,
won't ever reach, the floor. Carols seep
from the Hi-Fi. Baby hums along;
she already knows these songs.

It's a pretty time, isn't it? Everything's gold
and warm but Baby feels a strange
breaking someplace underneath.
It's in her skin, her spleen, liver, lungs.
She breathes it in; sings it out.

O come, O
come all ye, O.
Come, let us.
Come.

It, faithful, does stay.

First Transmission

In 1977, an entity calling themselves "Vrillon" created a broadcast interruption to a transmitter of the UK's Independent Broadcasting Authority. They delivered a warning for Earth citizens to remove their weapons of evil and learn to live together in peace.

Baby is the disaster
which threatens
your world,

and the voice
of the weapons

within you.

Round Baby Finds a Bullet in the Street

At first, she thinks
it's a turtle, elliptical,
tiny and smooth,
creeping from the median,
across the asphalt,
inching toward her
where she squats
on the hot sidewalk.

She opens her
palm to let it
climb on. *Come here,*
little cutie.
Let me feed you
seven kinds of lettuce
from Mother's fridge.

But wait—
look closer.
This morsel's
movement's mechanical,
inorganic.

Don't move, Baby.

It's heading over.
It's aiming, straight
and true.

Test Tube Baby

No, not a tube
like they keep saying

on TV. Flat dish
with low sides to keep

the juicy human fluid
from spilling over.

Slimy excited bits
swimming

circles until
they catch

something. Fishing
for faces, fingers,

meaty lips. I know
this isn't right

science talk.
But, Mother,

I'm a tube girl, too—
growing too large

for this shattered shape or any
calibrated laboratory glass.

Round Baby Runs Away

At the end of the block,
there's a bus stop,
no, a lamp post,
no, a mouse hole.

Baby, Baby, where
are you planning to go?

Stuff your bag
with provisions:
Matchbox cars,
Shaun Cassidy,
Skylab, Funyuns. Take

the busted umbrella because
Mother's always calling
for rain. Roll your socks
into tight round
stones. When your feet

get wet, go cold,
stretch them all the way
up and over, bind your top
to your bottom, keep your body
whole and warm and going.

Run, Baby. The street
is long and tree-less
and the summer sun
wants to eat you like
a sweet, fat plum.

Round Baby Rides the Landslide

"I'm part of that (expletive) mountain." —Harry Randall Truman, 1980

Baby wonders what it feels like,
the weight of ash on the tongue.

At what rate must it fall in order
to accumulate, dry as a gospel,

against wet flesh? Won't it dissolve
upon hitting hot mouth, breath

leaching slow as snowstorm from low
winter clouds? But it's May now, so

no snow except here at the highest
peaks. Baby's made her way up

the north face easily by grasping
and leaping, teasing stubborn

rock from empty air. When
she gets there she wants to dance

the backbone of the continent,
popping each vertebra

with her pumice stone toes,
until the world releases

all the worry and stress
that's been building for one

hundred twenty-seven years.
Below her now, the ground shrugs

forward and lets itself go
with a lateral blast. Baby

doesn't yet know the word
orgasm, still she's bound to it,

above it, inside, rides the landslide
down, through trees and trailer parks,

flattening cars and cattle and odd,
obstinate men raving in flimsy

cabins in the danger zone. Over
her head and behind her, the ash

column rises, forms a cloud
neither soft nor melting.

Baby looks back at the machine
of it, thrusting out and up,

a monstrous velocity
that outruns the sun.

Round Baby Imagines Ships Made of Steel and Stars

At night in her blue shag bedroom, Baby
plays a game. First, turn off the lights.
Now, feel your pupils dilate, widen,
welcome dark like a flood. There, above you,
the ceiling whirls like a world. Like a celestial
expanse. Imagine ships made of steel and stars.
Imagine looping through galaxies, alone. Space
is vast, Baby knows, and imagines her parents
nowhere inside of it. Press your eyes together
hard until colors appear on the thin skin screen
of your lids. Count *one, two, three*. Now open
them and picture Mother, Father, floating,
like astronauts tethered to the ship of you.
Three, two, one, now blink and send them scattering,
tumbling into cosmos, cut from the very world.

Round Baby Consents to Swear

What's your favorite animal, Baby?
Sister says *Red Panda*, says
cats we live with, 100%. Sister

makes you swear you love every
cat, bear, lizard, fish,
as much as you love your own

parents, as much as you love Sister,
yourself, and any children who may
lodge themselves in your someday

body, creatures cupped inside
what Father calls *your birthing hips.*
You consent to swear, but already

imagine fire flicking the walls,
smoke choking the air above
and all around your dumb blue

room. The cats jump from bed
to dresser to floor. They bat always
at the door. You'll be better

without them, Baby. Safe as houses out
on the street, so say you love them
just as much. Say you love them

even more.

Round Baby Dreams of Apples

Baby dreams of apples, red and gold,
plucked from high branches by her clunky
mitten hands. Sister sits in the muddy earth
beneath low limbs, munching on Empires,
Winesaps, Jona Gold. Three bites then pitches
them into the dirt path between orchard
rows. Baby crunches a tart green globe,
feels the sour rush, ugly, to her gut.
Another. Another. Mother warns her
toward temperance. Too many apples
will play havoc with your body, Baby.
Screw up your systems. Lay you out. Baby
eats everything, even the seeds, wonders
how long it will take a tree to root between
her liver and spleen. Frothy green limbs
tending toward blazing sun lungs.

Round Baby Watches the Sky for Falling Debris

"We assume that Skylab is on the planet Earth, somewhere."
—Charles S. Harlan, Skylab mission controller, July 1979

July blue, continental and hot
as asphalt, Everyone's
tuned to the news, waiting,
wondering where and when.
Baby itches in skin
stretched
like a too-tight
balloon, ready to pop.

Space can only hold so much.

Lift your face, Baby,
squint your eyes and watch
the sky for falling debris:

solar panel

        father

    heat shade

                 bedroom

metal hunks

bed

          hunger

               mother

               blood

    waste tank

    waist band   where is it   where is it   where will it

      fall

Second Transmission

We have watched your skies.

We are deeply concerned
your existence may be blessed.

This is the voice of Vrillon, a representative of the New Baby Age.

Round Baby's All Body

Bouncing Baby, strong-
gripped girl,
whirring, twirling, swallow,
and grow. Billow
and bound and bleed.

Eat.

Swim under
the ocean and out
of the way. Hide
in your closet. Stay. Open
the bathroom door.

Smudge your blood so
Mother can see.
Bend toward vortex.
Bruise your shins,
arms, flailing or pumping

like pistons. Baby
you're a fat little furnace,
a flesh engine
burning with syntax and symbols,
humming and stomach,

bursting hips
with plush lips
with wishes
and watching
and worry,

with will.

Round Baby Eats Apples Laced with Razor Blades

Mother doesn't know it's mostly a hoax. Cyanide
candies, LSD dosing, needles like peanuts
in chocolate bars. This is the world we
live in, and she's heard enough horror
stories to believe that evil sleeps inside us
all. She'll expect you to dump it out on the bed
before gorging yourself. She's only protecting
your throat, Baby, your clumped and choking soul.

It's time to get ready. You'll go out at dusk,
leafless trees after late rain, dark shapes ghosting
down the street as a pack, pumpkin glow, cold
but no coat to cover your soothsayer scarves, gold
hoop earrings, long skirt sodden and soaked.
You'll climb each staircase and prepare
your pillowcase. Ring each doorbell and pretend
your goldfish didn't leap to its near-death

this morning, out of the glass bowl
and onto the heating grate—like a city
sewer vent spewing from your family room
floor. You'll forget how you padded downstairs
for breakfast and stood barefoot on that burning
metal, skin blistering, the basement's foul breath
suggesting through your flannel nightdress. When
it got too hot you stepped off, back into your shivering

costume of skin. But there still lay your small dumb
pet. Forget how you saw its fin twitch and reached
to bring it back to breathing, but reached too far
and instead felt your finger flare with its own grim
thought, how you gritted your milk teeth and flicked it
through the waiting space between the beastly

grates. It's getting late, Baby. The porch lights on
your block blink off and your bag's full
of fruit, sour-juiced and seeping, sliced
through to the rotten core.

Round Baby Believes in Ghosts

—for Carol Anne

Baby believes in ghosts—of course
she does. She can feel if not
see their misty outlines, their heat
wave patterns rising from some
energy field, their once-corporal forms.

Baby's ghosts belong to her. Ancestral
and loving, she longs to touch
their slim-cheeked faces. Grandfather,
Great-grandmother. Father says
ghosts are just memories or wishes,

shifting pixels trapped inside
television screens. But Baby's all body

and belief. In her bed, under carnival mesh
that flutters and swirls, she stares
at the Day-Glo constellations and cries,

tries to conjure the scent of skin
and hair. Longs to loan her voice
to their scraped and soothing tones.

They call her from the bright pink
maw of the closet, *Baby, Baby, we're here.*

Round Baby Absorbs Her Classmates

Baby's getting rounder
by the day. Something growing

inside her. Someone starting
to make room. *You've got hips*

like battleships. An ass you could put
a map on. What? It's a compliment,

Baby! (Bitch.) Legs plush, belly billowing,
even her lips, that one boy said, *plump*

as pillows. Kissable and soft.
Baby has a choice to make: stuff this other

under peek-a-boo skin. Deny her girth, mirth.
Or, take all this delicious new

fat (ass) and fit it like a uniform,
let it (hips) squish against firm surfaces—

dressers, beds, the roof of the school &
other bolting bodies. Send it reeling, Baby;

set it loose and uncontained, bounding,
bouncing like a Super Ball, like that movie

Blob rolling grotesquely forward,
a ravenous metaphor absorbing your classmates,

the school bus, the biting
boys, your neighbors, their houses,

the street, sweet Sister, dim parents
and the whole dumb windowless world.

Round Baby Remembers How It Hovered & Hummed

Later, she will come to love the boy-muscle,
pretty skin over top of pink tension,
like a billion exclamation points bundled
inside a truncheon. What she remembers
of yours, cousin, is how it hovered there,
wrapped in white fibers, inside
the metal-dense atmosphere
of your parents' walk-in
closet. Baby remembers
how it hummed, rocket-hot
and revving below her grabbed
hand, perpendicular to propriety
and primed
to breach containment.

Round Baby's Mostly Human

Baby's legs work fine
on regular days.
Her eyes blink green
and seeking.
Salivary glands
active and alive.
In the anatomy book
of her body, the transparencies
proceed as one would expect:

Skeletal
Muscular
Endocrine
Cardiovascular
Nervous
Digestive
Excretory
Integumentary

(Clack, thrum, skin bristle, swallow, flush, flinch.)

She's mostly human, most
of the time. But there are those
moments when her connectors
seem scrambled. When, say,
Baby intends simply to lift
her head from the concrete
steps, or hold hard her breath. But
what she gets instead is gut
trouble, eye spasm, marrow cramp.

Or she'll think, *blush inside*
this embrace, small hairs rise,
but her synapse will say,
contract, and then Baby becomes
an origami project, small folds
into smaller folds,

until she is one thousand
paper cranes hanging
inside a grimy market
window, granting herself
her own somatic wish.

Round Baby Bakes a Cake

It's nobody's birthday
but Baby bakes
a cake anyway.
She likes to feed

people, loves to watch their
faces blush with hunger,
then melt into stuffed and sated
relief. Their puffed cheeks.

Baby reads the recipe and gathers
her ingredients: flour, sugar,
milk and eggs. Vanilla. Mixing
bowl. Whisk.

Wait, Baby.
What flavor?

Sister would say *pink*
and mean Hubba Bubba bubble
gum—something sticky and choking
sweet. Father's favorite's carrot,
spiked with cinnamon and derision,
crowned with sour cream.

(Silly Baby, Mother doesn't eat cake.)

You'd rather have chocolate, bitter
as embarrassment, dark and dour,
sticking to your hips. Stir
everything together until all

your luscious lumps dissolve and pour
into a metal pan. Bake for fourteen
years at whatever temperature
will crisp the edges, blister

the surface, scorch your sugar
till it shines like strawberry

Lipsmacker on shards
of mirror glass.

Round Baby Says Father, Says Falling

Baby remembers her dream again,
rolls to her notebook first thing
to snatch it with a pen. She's read
it's a way of staying, of saving
before the melt of morning. This dream,

like all dreams, met
her in the middle. Doubles
and pairs but not twins. Near
but not matching, un-mirrored:

grapefruit spoons : tumors
spongy lungs : porcelain plate
reticulated : river
blister : bladder

farther : Father
thinks dreams
are boring, dull rummage
of diurnal input. But Baby loves
their bluster, tries to show him
the landscape inside
her night mind. Says: *Father*

says *falling/*
says menacing braid/ pink blade/ household
appliance /says plastic/ says
broken bridge, drive
over pine trees, flying/
says ugly/such a long dream/says
comet/says trying I'm trying I'm trying/
too alive

Round Baby Pivots & Bursts

The gym floor's slick
and nobody's watching so
Baby twirls in sweater tights,
gathering static with every
twist. A scrawling
proclamation, gyroscopic
chaos, hot and faster, around
she goes and when she stops
the whole gym glows
like an ember. Baby pivots
and bursts from her uniform skirt,
blue plaid sparks spray as she spins
like a pencil, ground down
and sharpened to a beautiful, brutal
point.

Round Baby Liquefies & Digests

Baby takes her shower as hot
as possible, prefers to emerge
pink and steaming. Flayed.

Mornings she stays in the spray,
flirts with pain, flesh
scrubbed and sloughed,

Small hairs rousing as from
desire or disgust. What will it
feel like to transform?

Today Baby clogs her going,
stanches the flow with a filthy cloth.
Crouches down in an inch

of tepid water, black hairs
unlatched and floating,
held in thrall by her own wet web.

Her face elongates in the gleam of spigot,
slims as if stretched by some brute
mechanism of anxiety. Father. Lunchroom.

Cousin. Bra strap. Breast bud. Bus.
Whose terror can she liquefy and digest?
What makes everyone jump?

Abdomen distending, Baby extends
maxillae to mouthpart and tries to feel
warm. Chitinous particles of cuticle bristle

in the dank water sucking her into the whirlpool at the drain.
But even now Baby can hold her breath tight. Legs fold under
Her one at a time for the flush through the sewer pipe.

She's a jumper, a burrower, a wolf—will not be washed out.
Baby crawls into your mouth when you sleep.
Outside she pulls birds from the sky.

Third Transmission

Have no fear, Baby.
We thank you
for your energy.

(You can be so sensitive.
We are speaking to you!)

Round Baby Climbs to the Roof of the School

Shoes off,
toes tucked
like mortar
up, up,
hand over
hand. Finger
tip skin rips
against cool,
dark brick.
Baby climbs,
clever as
a spider,
silk-quiet,
and stealth. Lugs
muscles, lungs up
and away
from the play-
ground below:
You know what
we're gonna do
to you, Baby?

Gang
        bang.

Keep going.

Those dopes
don't know
the lush of
language, Baby,
the danger and delight
of getting a word

just
        right.

Tonight, you
climb outside

semantics, scale
your own
scaffolding,
the words
we learn
to skirt

      (avoid
      a one-piece
      garment not
      joined between
      the legs)

or launch
          (load
    release)

a volley
              (a discharge

       an outpouring

    a burst)

a salvo
      (excuse or
         evasion

        concentrated fire

        something to soothe
    a person's reputation

a rising,

    rousing

    round

of applause.)

Territory

I lick
my way
across hot
wires, over
slick teeth,
wrap myself
around tube-
socked calves.
The desk pressing
into my back.
In social studies
class we are
studying some war.
Muscles tight.
Tongue. Tongue.
This is
not the first
mouth but
I will say it
is, later. I will
claim it.
The border walls collapse
into themselves
when not in use.
We kiss
like the enemies we are,
out in the open
without cover
or partition.

Round Baby Turns up the Record Player

Don't borrow trouble,
Baby. Nobody knows
what's swirling
inside your dirty
mind. Mother thinks
she reads signs inscribed
on your thighs—purpled
stretch marks she mistakes
for backtalk, bold blood.
She's wrong about you.
When she comes to the shut
door of your room, pretend
you're not in there, slicking
your lips to that boy. Say,
Simulating earth worm dissection,
or
Listening to Twisted Sister.

Stay hungry, Baby.

Turn up the record player
and let her believe you.

She will—
for a little while.

Round Baby Sees Skies Filled with Dark Circles

Baby's worried
about
The Bomb
now.
On TV,
singing
in the
background,
the men
and ladies
with helmet
hair use words
like *glasnost,*
perestroika,
détente.
Baby listens
to pop songs
about parents
in Russia who love
their children,
about red
balloons lifting
into the sky,
the opposite
of fallout.
Cartoon bombs
are always
round and black
with a white
cotton wick
that gets lit
futilely, somewhere
in the desert.
Baby knows,
because
of TV,
that this bomb,
The Bomb,

her bomb, takes
a different shape.
But in her mind
she sees
skies filled
with dark
circles, like
periods
at the
end of
sentences,
raining
down
down.

Designer

these jeans are all wrong
not allowed to wear acid wash
designer
Father says painted-on
Jordache Sergio Valente Sassoon
make my ass look huge
but I'm good at this

better than good

do you love me yet
band boy
with your embouchure and my
mouth mouth mouth mouth mouth

Chameleons

wicked words every day baby touch it he said he's in my jeans better
than anyone I come and go I come and he said you know your lips
are really soft baby pillow soft and pulls my hair back stage he put
his hands there heard me say he said I know you better than said why
don't you leave him everyone knows and you used to be so sweet

Round Baby Hisses & Spits

Baby's bored with bodies,
sick of the record's rotation:
obvious hard-on or
Spandexed suggestion--
take your pick.
Sweet cheap harmony.
Stuff it in 'til it fits.

What's gonna happen when that one
comes strutting down the hallway,
all swagger and glam? Chorus
of twitchy fingers and door-knob knees
lick of metal and sweaty lips,
wailing blue-balled need

look at those hips, hips, hips, lips…

[bridge]

They never do ask you, really.
Never nudge their bulge
against you just so.

Their love don't wait for you, Baby.
Just shred solo, jump split
from the sticky, glittering stage

Oh Baby,
blow me, baby
in the band room,
behind the stairwell door,
in the back of my mom's blue
station wagon…

Psych!

Monotony's got its own
soundtrack. You've heard this
jam before: big-haired power

ballad, eyeliner- slick,
leggy car-straddle
of that MTV chick.

[here we go again]

Do it as usual, Baby,
suck it hard and quick,
kneeling next to
the woodwinds
which also hiss and spit.

baby baby baby baby
baby baby yeah
baby god gimme
baby oh baby yeah yeah yeah yeah yeah yeah
yeah yeah yeah yeah yeah yeah yeah yeah

[fade out]

Fourth Transmission

Sisters! You may now proceed
to accept or reject the suck but
Baby exists to pass on the light
from planet Earth.

We warn you about your skies.

Round Baby Screams at the Idiot Children

*"I wonder who was spared? I wonder if New York, Paris, Moscow...
are just like Kansas City now?"*
—The Day After, ABC Television, November 20, 1983

It's the same dream
Baby's had for weeks
since seeing the movie
where children survive
the blast, only to throw open
the shelter doors the day after

and sprint into atomic wind.
They can't be held in.
Another fallow field spotted
with dying livestock.
Dark sky hot with particles,
dim flick of chill sun.

Everything's ending again,
and the scene doesn't change,
never shifts. This isn't
snow. No lilting drift
of early spring,

a light coat thrown over
the shoulders on your way
out to play. Baby's locked in
her dream-brain watching
everything unfold. She knows
how the next part goes:

dart left, then right, then jump
over felled meat shells, ash
piling high on their hides,
into their loosening hair.
Soon their skin will begin

to blister, their systems clump
then crumble to dust.

It isn't snow! Baby screams
at the idiot children. *Suck
back your dumb swelling tongues!*

Round Baby Barks Orders into the Hot Wind

Secure your face.

Blink a dark blockade.

Don't take your eyes off.

Drink what you pour.

Fix your digestion.

Stop dropping your R's.

Roll over.

Get off my propensity.

Open your coat.

Leave that poor boy that poor boy that poor boy alone.

Figure me up.

Face the window.

Finish your plying.

Fail to see.

Leave the meat.

Don't speak to your fixture like that.

Don't suck so hard.

Hurry.

Hurry.

Stroll into the vortex.

Get out of the way.

Round Baby Displaces

Pick the biggest tube, Baby,
rubber skin, thick and black
as licorice that squeaks against
your teeth. Sweet water. Settle in.
The river, clear for the first
time in weeks, rises perceptibly
when you enter it, displacing tadpoles
and algae, spilling its muddy,
minnowed banks. This, Baby, is your truest
shape. Not really round after all,
but tubular—a hollow where your meat
should be. Clouds gather and crayfish
nip at your thick, callused toes.
Thunder, distant still, but coming close.

Round Baby, Dissolved Upon Lift-Off

"If you're offered a seat on a rocket ship, don't ask what seat. Just get on."
—Christa McAuliffe, 1986

Baby stayed home from school, cramps like hot spikes
inside, heating pad strapped to her gut like an engine.
Today she hates having a body. But isn't she milking
it a little. She wanted to watch—what does she love
more than celestial spectacle?—but not crammed around
a wheeled-in TV during English class, those close-reading
mouth-breathers jamming the static field sparking
from screen. (What does she love more than a room set-ablaze
with misunderstanding?) Baby needs space to consider
velocity, trajectory, how badly she wants to learn how
to leave. At home, she shares position with the Florida launch
audience: all of them staring up from the tarmac, eyes
like hole-punched paper, bright fluttering void. Baby cranes
her face to her own drop-ceiling sky— crumbling acoustic
tile, pink fiberglass she wants to pluck at and let
the slivers breach her bloodstream. She wants to think
about how that would work. Would it be a quick journey,
73 seconds between brain and heart? How high
will they reach? And would Baby have taken that teacher's
place? Maybe. She knows the tropopause—can both see it
and see *through* it to a higher space, a realm beyond
her own dull knowing. What's above beseeches, clever
and technical, but there's just no way to reach it.
Baby falls back to her watch spot on the couch
in time to feel the shiver, the thrust and burst
of brightest flight. They're gone now, Baby,
dissolved upon lift-off: low plume of white, barest
branch framed against frantic blue sky, goodbye.

Round Baby Grabs Her Scalpel

Baby wakes up early. Outside still
looks like a negative, a reversal,
dun colored, world of dull dark.

The trees in the park should be green
soon, black iris up next
to the crumbling front steps.

The house is quiet but she
can hear the whisper-small
sounds of growth through

the cracks in the windows,
the gaps around the doors.
The air outside is cool,

the kitchen, chilled. Baby finds
the fridge filled with eggs
of all sizes, in every hue. White,

brown, blue. She plucks one
from Styrofoam, and brings
it to the sink. Thinks

about how this season's meant
to ring loud as church bells,
fill the world with light.

Mother might say the word,
saved, but Baby would bristle,
then blush. She shakes the egg

in her warm hand then holds
it still. Grabs her scalpel
and pierces the shallow end.

Worries the tip back and forth until
a crack forms and the shell
gives way. Careful, careful.

Just a bit of yolk, Baby. Be gentle,
Be sure. Now put your lips against
the fat end, and blow

like you're praying, blow
while the morning shivers,
while the whole world rises
and glows.

Round Baby Boils the Bones

At the kitchen table,
Baby tears at roasted chicken
from the grocery store,
pulling limp skin loose.
It's mid-afternoon
and sister's in her bedroom,
squirming beneath a boy she blew
at school. No sound coming
out of there, but Baby knows.
Fingers to greasy lips, she feeds
herself though she's not hungry for
once. The white meat separates

easily from the breast plate,
slides off in one long chunk
she can shred. In a few years,
Sister will escape, fly through
an open window, grabbing at
skin as she goes. When all the flesh
comes off the bird, Baby will boil
the bones for soup
and for jewelry—wishbone
strung like a brittle pendant
from the ripcord hanging
loosely at her neck.

Round Baby Pours Down as Black Rain

She swims through the cooling tubes
waiting for the gap in the system,
for the shift to change, the men to get
a little lazy like men do. Baby's
made for a moment like that. A sliver,

a splinter, a blink and you'll miss it.
It only takes a second to heat
herself far beyond fixing.

She's an uncontrolled
reactor/reaction.
A level-7 meltdown coming
to a town near you!

Steam explosion and open-air fire,
Baby's damage goes deep to the core,
and rises in the air above Pripyat.
Isotope Baby pours down
as black rain over Belarus
and Ukraine. Cesium,
Strontium, Iodine, little bits
of Baby radiate as far away as the Alps.

In the village, a wedding band
and a vegetable garden and someone's
fishing in the river, still. The State
delays the way states do. Classical
music swims through radio speakers,
conditioning citizens to hear some version
of the emergency: Baby's gone

but also inside every living thing
for miles. Boar bristle, fingernail,
fish cheek, cow hide. Find her
residue thriving 30 years,
70 years, 3,000 years from now.
In the Red Forest, in the nervous
birds. In the dogs missed by bullets.

In whatever creatures follow
from the brown bear and the lynx,

inside the exclusion zone
guarding every glowing thing
we left behind.

Fifth Transmission

Baby, you are a part light,
part weapons. Proceed
to deeply concerned.

In your existence, the destiny of Earth.
You must learn Confusion, Chaos and Untruth.
Learn the Sun.

This is the voice of the planet as it passes
into disaster.

I'm a Loaded Gun

after I didn't come you did Doritos

then homework

yes, school in my bedroom, my skin

Ash Wednesday's for fasting and abstinence

(of course I didn't)

no church girl anymore

my own room dumb numb and open

your shudder

you give slick sin

but I do this to myself

whoa, there's chains in what you sell

oh what the hell

(of course I'm too young)

I'm saved by my body the damage is done

Round Baby Makes of Herself a Pyre

Nobody Baby knows celebrates Solstice.
The dark just comes and then it goes.
But this year she wants to mark it, make it

somehow her own. Into the woods behind
the shed she goes to collect sticks and dry twigs.
There's the tree she was climbing

the first time she bled. High branch split
like a switch, she could feel her sludge
issue forth, burn through brittle bark.

How she tensed her legs and lodged
there, sluiced and throbbing
in the hot crotch of it.

But that was years ago. Tonight, Baby claims
an armful of cold kindling to make of herself
a pyre, a place where dark words burn.

Squid. Dweeb. Weirdo. Nerd.
Baby face. Crybaby. Loser. Girl.

Baby's made from language and tree
skin, girl bark, finger root and earth
meat, see? She rubs thick thighs together,

leans them up, one against
the other so they smoke and spew
like static that flew from sweater tights

in the bathroom where she doused herself
to drown the spark, stanch the flow.
Gather your limbs up tight, Baby,

and strike the match. Time to go.
Stars shine like knife points
above the trees, the shed,

your broiling, brilliant wooden head.

Round Baby Creeps around Her Clouded Cortex

swirl of angst
grey funk descending
like November   error
error can't

remember what it was she was
supposed to be
thinking   Baby creeps
around her clouded

                  cortex snapping synapse

misfire   hello eyelids   like piano
keys plink plink help
her make sense see through

         haze this ice-glazed
window at the top of her brain
up up bust
         it bare fist
her smarts swallow
this figment fixture

it's in her

ear her near

nightmare aware   hey there
there there   now   halting
               at the edge of ordinary

terror

Round Baby Slips on Her Sexy

Baby's stuck inside a cricket cage.
Got caught and can't get out.
It was bound to happen, Baby,
how you slipped on your sexy
exoskeleton. Fun dress-up,
such drag. All that light chirping
from your fingertips. Be glad
they found you out
there. God knows where
you thought you were going.
Pull your swollen ovipositor
back from the ready ground.
Lift your leg to sing.

Round Baby Plunders the Orange Sky

"Look, Doris. Like, I'm 18, okay? And I can watch the comet wherever I want to watch the comet."
—Night of the Comet, Paramount Pictures, 1984

The comet's coming close tonight.
Baby's been tracking the sky,
watching through fogged binoculars
for the periodic show—dirty ice
and gas wrapped around the horizon
like a loose winter scarf. The first time

she looked up, she waited for space
metal that would miss her and fall
on Australia. Months earlier, her parents
let her bang pots with wooden spoons
on the front stoop at New Year's, under
a dark dome of cold. *Watch. Watch.*
Wait. Maybe it will be early, Baby

thought. Maybe it will come crashing down.
Now, here, years later, everyone's craning
their faces up, a whole lot of ga-ga
over the comet's certain return.
Baby's tired of the craze. This public
lust for Halley's kept her grouchy

for days. There's no astronomy club
at school, just anatomy and physiology
where that teacher shaped like a rectangle
chucked a rheumy sheep's eye at her head.
Dissection time is now! he clanged. It bounced
and Baby drew her scalpel follicle-close. So grody.

No, the heavens are what hold her, always
have. Ten days ago, seven gorgeous sparks
flew from a thick white rocket plume
into the Florida blue. Baby sees them
now as stitches, sewn into the skin

of night. The word for this is *wound*.
She shudders and spurns the nerd-

boys, jocks and dirtbags amassing in paneled
basements around town to pound
lukewarm cans of Coors, the official spectacle
beverage, and listen to Boston blast their dumb
invitation to enter. *We're ready C'mon!* But
Baby really is ready now. She's Reggie

Belmont, B-movie-ready to bash comet
zombies in the brain with heavy wrenches,
then go shopping with Sister at Benetton.
Ready to be beautiful and brutal, humanity's last
line of defense. What would it feel like to breathe
that red haze that was Father, Mother,

and stagger into the next empty day? Media
says Halley's a dim dud, a burnt bulb.
Such disappointment. A total bust. *Ooh ooh.*
Still, Baby feels like there's something
just out of sight, other side of the sun,
so she plunders the orange sky
for arrival or exit sign. She'll be 90 in 2061.

Round Baby Orients Herself by the Glow

In the constellated dark, Baby heads into the thicket,
treks miles out to find her way back in. Too many stars
and none of them home. Baby speaks answers
into the air and waits for a marker to appear:
in the forest, on the roof, don't go in there, float

Which part of longing is kindness? Which bile?
How can you feel lousy about light? Go to bed,
Baby, here on the hoary ground. Park your pack
by the side of the road and when sun comes see

who'll stop if you use your mouth. This way,
that way, where ya going, girlie? Orient yourself
by the glow of lightning bugs and billboards.
By the sound of gravel grinding like teeth in thin sleep.

Round Baby Collects around the Edges

Round Baby's brisket simmers
on the stovetop, stink of pickling
spice and peppercorn. Beige
scum collects around the edges
of the blue iron pot.
Who will come to the table
to snag this sinew
when it's finished?
Who will hold the gelatinous fat
that slides between fork tines
as she slices in and against the grain?
Whose teeth will need picked clean?

Baby's tired of cooking for herself
now that everyone else has left
for the event horizon without her.
Lonely girl, un-hungry, lucky for the hours
it will be before this ugly supper's done.

Round Baby Chews Her Own Arm Off to Get Away

God gave
you teeth,
Baby,
so by God,
use them.

Sixth Transmission

Sisters, you are free
now that we are here

and weapons of Baby exist.

You are now leaving
the disaster, the higher
stages of removed.

We order that you light
the dross within you.

You will share in the Great Goodwill.

Round Baby Hip-Checks the Charming Abyss

Baby feels pulled toward orbits beyond
the scope of her own knowing. Black holes
roiling at the center of her galaxy, static
sound of a neutron star, recorded for broadcast
on NOVA. She dreams in nebulae, Halley's comet
streaking across her night mind. Space
is where she belongs, Baby knows.

She's failing physics though,
(too much band room sucking?)
so she's stayed stuck to the thin scrim
of earth. That's not true. She never
even took it. Never tried.
(too many fingers inside?) Can't tell

you anything about the states of matter,
laws of motion, general relativity,
trajectory of time. How are stars born?
Why so many lies? And what happens
to a body, Baby, here at the event horizon?
Strut toward it, all thrust and bulge
and sway, and let it pull you along

the elongated axis of your terror, hip-check
the charming abyss. Hot glow at the top
of your head says *Let's go! Time to pull
your constituent atoms apart! Spaghettify
your cells!* It's your pool party, Baby,

so pencil-dive, lithe and gorgeous
toward the sexy singularity, become
yourself, twinned: dendritic impulse,
reaching neural ray. Exploratory
and arboreal. Infinite and inevitable.
(How much they couldn't know.)

Step forward, Baby.
Follow her in. Watch
yourself go.

Gratitude

Writing this book felt like a fun and mysterious adventure even as it was also cathartic and empowering for me, and, I hope, maybe for you, too. Round Baby is not me, in case you're wondering, though we are roughly the same age and have had many of the same experiences. If you know me, you may feel like arguing this point by reminding me of the time my navy-blue sweater tights did actually send static shooting like stars, or the time I got caught in my bedroom with one particular boy or another. To this I will say, okay but I never got to be a cricket or a spider or a radioactive isotope or a sharpened pencil tip or the Blob. Things might have been easier for me if I had. Adolescence is just mostly terrible. Terrible for me in the 80s, worrying about nuclear war, terrible for my kids in the 2020s, worrying about global warming. We should all have some superpowers, an extra pair of legs or three, really sharp teeth, an open window, a comet we can hop on, just out of sight. If not, then we should at least have great friends. I may have had terrible hair, but I had great friends in the 80s and they are inside these poems, too. So…

Thank you, Gabby, Shannon, Susan, Laura, Laura, Andrea, Jane, Brooke, Nicole, Jen and Claudia. I'm also lucky to have great friends now. I didn't know them in the 80s but if I had…you know, I have no idea what *Breakfast Club*-like configuration we would have made, but they have been Baby's cheering section since the beginning. Thank you, Brittany Hailer, Joy Katz, Dave Housley, Sherrie Flick, Sarah Shotland, Sandra Faulkner & Joel Patton. Thank you to Heidi Czerwiec, Su Cho, Kelly Boyker Guillemette, Patty Paine, Allison Joseph and John Tribble, and all the editors who have loved her and given her shape on the pages of their journals, and to the press editors and contest judges who gave her enough encouragement that I kept sending her out. Thank you so much to the BrickHouse Books team— Clarinda, Doritt, Ace and judge Katherine Young for believing in and blessing this book. I'm so glad she's finally found her home with you. Thank you to Kerstin Rünzel for creating the astonishing cover art that gave Baby one of her many forms. Thank you to my Pittsburgh writing community for inviting me to read these poems over the years and to my colleagues and students at Chatham University for their support as well. Thank you to my dear friend Julia Spicher Kasdorf for telling me these are persona poems. How'd I miss that? Thank you to Kelly

Cressio-Moeller who read this book in its final version and told me it unfolded like a David Lynch film. Thank you finally and forever to my husband, Paul, who wooed me 18 years ago with his love of apocalyptic and off-kilter narratives (among other things) and who read the first full draft and said, "This is really creepy, Sheil. I love it!" Thanks to my kids, Josie & Rudy, who also seem to appreciate (or at least tolerate) my odd aesthetic sensibilities, and to my mother and sister who may wonder what the hell is wrong with me but smile and nod uncomfortably anyway.

So, where did Baby go at the end? My Very Scientific Son says she couldn't possibly "still be out there," but I like to imagine that maybe she found a wormhole that let her skip her crappy 20s and landed her in a better timeline, a little later on, where she got to have a wonderful family and dogs and live in a lush green Rust Belt city where the rivers are pristine and the air is not poison and write poetry books. A world where people believe in science and trust in journalists, where boys and men and politicians fight as hard to undo sexism and misogyny as girls and women do; where maybe her father is still alive and one of those men, and a smart, capable, compassionate, take-no-shit woman has finally ascended to the highest political office in the land.

I like to imagine a world like that for her.

Acknowledgments

Atticus Review: "Round Baby Grabs Her Scalpel."

Bayou Magazine: "Round Baby Consents to Swear."

Broadsided Press: "Round Baby Sees Ships Made of Steel and Stars."

Crab Orchard Review: "Round Baby Rides the Landslide," "Round Baby Plunders an Orange Sky."

Diode: "Round Baby Sees Skies Filled with Dark Circles," "Fourth Transmission."

Fiolet & Wing Domestic Fabulism Anthology: "Round Baby Absorbs Her Classmates"

Grimoire: "Round Baby Liquefies & Digests."

Indiana Review: "Round Baby Hangs On No Matter How," "Round Baby Slips on Her Sexy," "Round Baby Feels a Strange Breaking."

Menacing Hedge: "Round Baby Pivots & Bursts," "Round Baby Pronounces & Proclaims," "Round Baby Boils the Bones," "Round Baby Orients Herself by the Glow," "Round Baby Can't Taste It Yet," "Round Baby Dreams of Apples."

North Dakota Quarterly: "Round Baby Finds a Bullet in the Street," "Round Baby Climbs to the Roof of the School," "Round Baby Believes in Ghosts," "Round Baby Runs Away."

Potluck: "Round Baby Eats Apples Laced with Razor Blades."

Stirring: A Literary Collection: "Round Baby Reaches Toward Interstitial Space."